W9-BRM-032

Sarcosuchus Imperator

by Daniel Cohen

Consultant:
Larry Dean Martin, Ph.D.
Professor-Senior Curator
Natural History Museum and Biodiversity Research Center
University of Kansas, Lawrence, Kansas

Bridgestone Books
an imprint of Capstone Press
Mankato, Minnesota

Bridgestone Books are published by Capstone Press
151 Good Counsel Drive, P.O. Box 669, Mankato, Minnesota 56002
www.capstonepress.com

Library of Congress Cataloging-in-Publication Data
Cohen, Daniel, 1936–
    Sarcosuchus Imperator / by Daniel Cohen.
    p. cm.—(Discovering dinosaurs)
    Summary: Introduces what is known of the physical characteristics, behavior, and habitat of
this reptile that lived during the time of dinosaurs.
    Includes bibliographical references and index.
    ISBN 0-7368-2525-8 (hardcover)
    1. Sarcosuchus imperator—Juvenile literature. [1. Sarcosuchus imperator. 2. Crocodiles,
Fossil. 3. Crocodiles.] I. Title.
QE862.C8C64 2004
567.9'8—dc22   2003012379

Editorial Credits
Amanda Doering, editor; Linda Clavel, series designer; Enoch Peterson, cover production
        designer and illustrator; Alta Schaffer, photo researcher; Karen Risch, product planning editor

Photo Credits
Corbis/Reuters NewMedia Inc., 4
Karen Carr, 8
Mike Hettwer, courtesy of Project Exploration, cover, 1, 10, 14, 18
Natural History Museum, 6
Paul Sereno, courtesy of Project Exploration, 12
Todd Marshall, www.marshalls-art.com, 16

1 2 3 4 5 6 09 08 07 06 05 04

Table of Contents

Sarcosuchus imperator compared to a
5-foot-tall (1.5-meter-tall) human

Sarcosuchus Imperator

Sarcosuchus imperator (SAR-koh-soo-kus IM-peer-AH-tor) was a giant **crocodile** that lived at the same time as dinosaurs. Sarcosuchus grew up to 40 feet (12 meters) long. It weighed 8.5 tons (8 metric tons). *Sarcosuchus imperator* means "flesh crocodile emperor."

emperor
a male ruler

The World of Sarcosuchus

Sarcosuchus lived 110 million years ago in northern Africa. Today, this area is the Sahara **Desert**. The climate was not dry in sarcosuchus' time. This area was covered with plants and water. Sarcosuchus lived in large rivers.

climate
the usual weather in a place

Deinosuchus

8

Relatives of Sarcosuchus

Scientists believe the first crocodiles lived 200 million years ago. Many types of crocodiles have lived since then. Deinosuchus (DIE-noh-SOO-kus) was a relative of sarcosuchus. Deinosuchus lived in North America.

Sarcosuchus imperator

Orinoco crocodile

Today's Crocodiles

Sarcosuchus is not directly related to today's crocodiles, but they look similar. Some of today's crocodiles are large, but none are as big as sarcosuchus. Today's largest crocodiles are half the length of sarcosuchus. Crocodiles today grow to be 20 feet (6 meters) long.

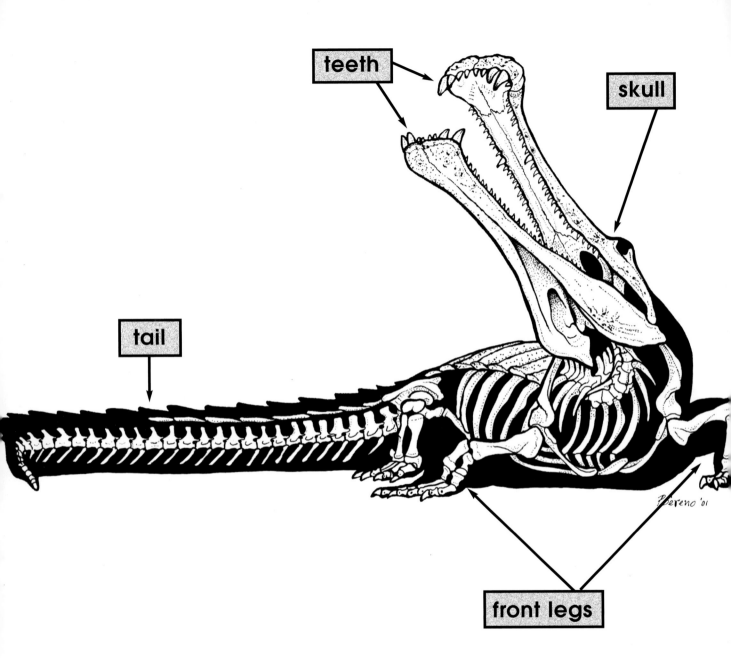

teeth

skull

tail

front legs

12

Parts of Sarcosuchus

Sarcosuchus looked much like crocodiles do today. It had a huge head. Its skull was almost 6 feet (2 meters) long. Sarcosuchus had a thick, wide body and short legs. Its tail was long and thick. Sarcosuchus' back was covered by tough plates.

Giant Jaws

Sarcosuchus' jaws took up almost its entire skull. The powerful jaws could crush bone. Sarcosuchus' jaws held at least 130 sharp teeth. Some of these teeth were 4 inches (10 centimeters) long.

16

What Sarcosuchus Ate

Sarcosuchus was a **carnivore**. It ate other animals. It ate almost any animal that it could catch. Sarcosuchus ate mostly fish. It also fed on turtles, lizards, and small dinosaurs.

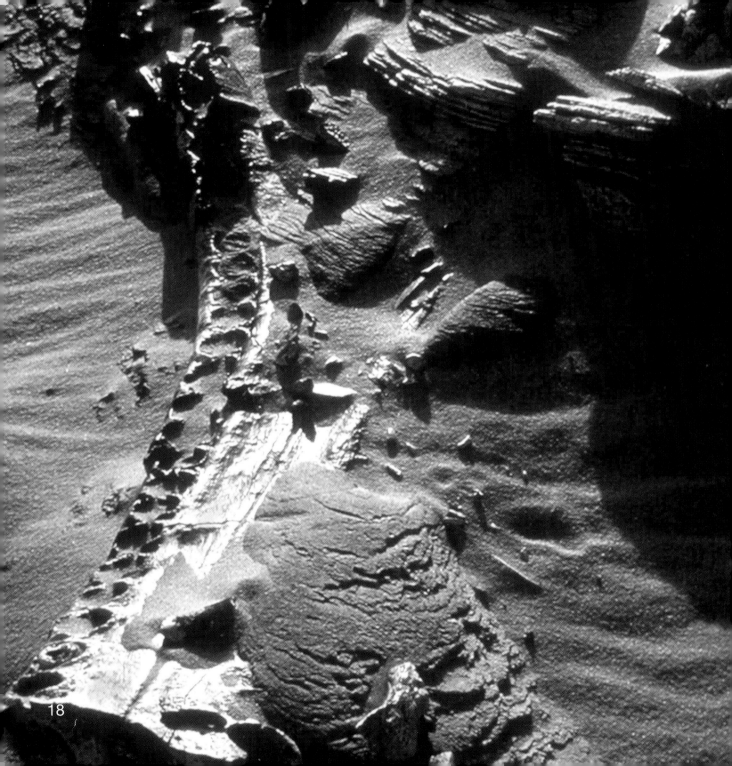

18

End of Sarcosuchus

Sarcosuchus died out long before the dinosaurs became **extinct**. Scientists are not sure why sarcosuchus became extinct. Some types of crocodiles survived whatever killed the dinosaurs. About 23 types of crocodiles still live on Earth.

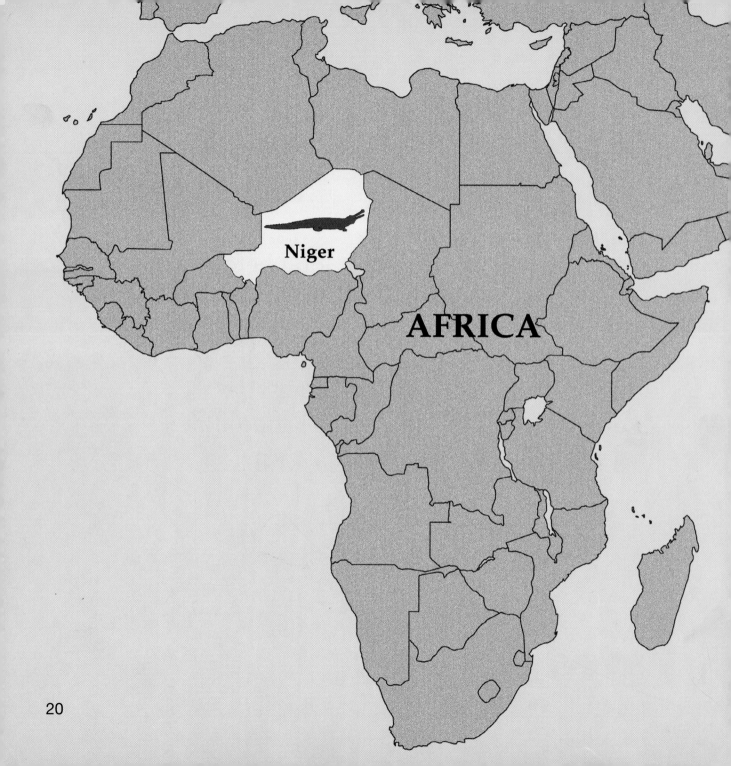

Niger

AFRICA

Discovering Sarcosuchus

   Sarcosuchus **fossils** were first found in the 1940s. In 2000, paleontologist Paul Sereno made a huge find in Niger, Africa. Sereno found a nearly complete sarcosuchus skull. He also found enough bones to know what the crocodile looked like.

paleontologist
a person who finds and studies fossils

Hands On: Comparing Crocodiles

Sarcosuchus grew to twice the length of today's largest crocodiles. Try this activity to see the difference between a Nile crocodile and sarcosuchus.

What You Need

3 friends
large open space
50-foot (15-meter) tape measure

What You Do

1. Stand back to back with a friend. The two other friends should stand back to back next to you and your friend.
2. You and your friend take 15 steps forward, heel to toe, moving away from each other.
3. Turn around and face your friend. This length is about how long a Nile crocodile can grow to be.
4. The two other friends take 30 steps forward, heel to toe, moving away from each other.
5. The two other friends turn around to face each other. This length is about how long sarcosuchus grew to be.
6. Measure the distance between your two friends. Is it close to 40 feet (12 meters)? What else is as long as sarcosuchus?

Glossary

carnivore (KAR-nuh-vor)—an animal that eats only meat

crocodile (KROK-uh-dile)—a large, scaly reptile with short legs and strong jaws

desert (DEZ-urt)—a dry area with little rain

extinct (ek-STINGKT)—no longer living anywhere in the world

fossil (FOSS-uhl)—the remains of something that was once alive; bones and footprints can be fossils.

Read More

Sloan, Christopher. *Supercroc and the Origin of Crocodiles.* Washington, D.C.: National Geographic, 2002.

Welsbacher, Anne. *Crocodiles.* Predators in the Wild. Mankato, Minn.: Capstone Press, 2003.

Internet Sites

FactHound offers a safe, fun way to find Internet sites related to this book. All of the sites on FactHound have been researched by our staff.

Here's how:
1. Visit *www.facthound.com*
2. Type in this special code **0736825258** for age-appropriate sites. Or enter a search word related to this book for a more general search.
3. Click on the Fetch It button.

FactHound will fetch the best sites for you!

Index

DATE			